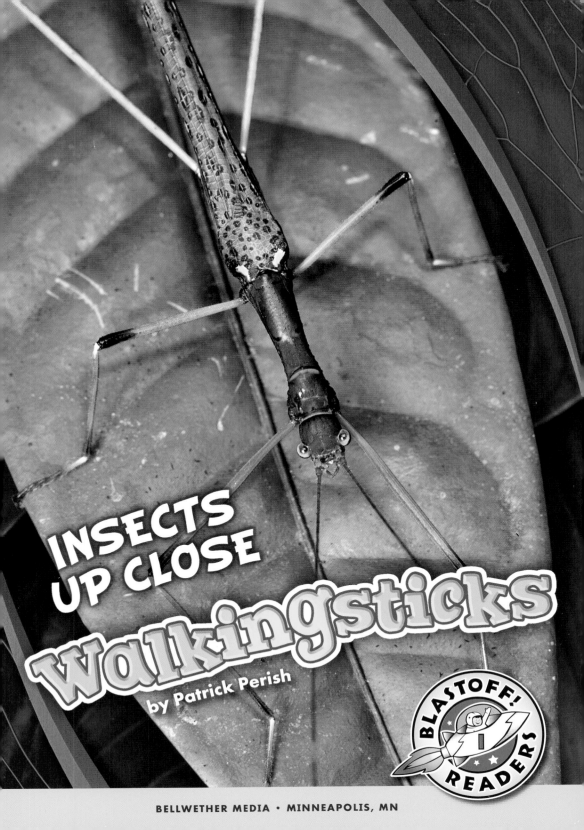

INSECTS UP CLOSE

Walkingsticks

by Patrick Perish

BELLWETHER MEDIA • MINNEAPOLIS, MN

Note to Librarians, Teachers, and Parents:

Blastoff! Readers are carefully developed by literacy experts and combine standards-based content with developmentally appropriate text.

Level 1 provides the most support through repetition of high-frequency words, light text, predictable sentence patterns, and strong visual support.

Level 2 offers early readers a bit more challenge through varied simple sentences, increased text load, and less repetition of high-frequency words.

Level 3 advances early-fluent readers toward fluency through increased text and concept load, less reliance on visuals, longer sentences, and more literary language.

Level 4 builds reading stamina by providing more text per page, increased use of punctuation, greater variation in sentence patterns, and increasingly challenging vocabulary.

Level 5 encourages children to move from "learning to read" to "reading to learn" by providing even more text, varied writing styles, and less familiar topics.

Whichever book is right for your reader, Blastoff! Readers are the perfect books to build confidence and encourage a love of reading that will last a lifetime!

This edition first published in 2019 by Bellwether Media, Inc.

No part of this publication may be reproduced in whole or in part without written permission of the publisher. For information regarding permission, write to Bellwether Media, Inc., Attention: Permissions Department, 6012 Blue Circle Drive, Minnetonka, MN 55343.

Library of Congress Cataloging-in-Publication Data

Names: Perish, Patrick, author.
Title: Walkingsticks / by Patrick Perish.
Description: Minneapolis, MN : Bellwether Media, Inc., [2019] | Series: Blastoff! Readers: Insects Up Close | Includes bibliographical references and index.
Identifiers: LCCN 2017056258 (print) | LCCN 2017058892 (ebook) | ISBN 9781626178045 (hardcover : alk. paper | ISBN 9781681035291 (ebook)
Subjects: LCSH: Stick insects--Juvenile literature.
Classification: LCC QL509.5 (ebook) | LCC QL509.5 .P47 2018 (print) | DDC 595.7/29--dc23
LC record available at https://lccn.loc.gov/2017056258

Editor: Christina Leaf   Designer: Tamara JM Peterson

Printed in the United States of America, North Mankato, MN

Table of Contents

What Are Walkingsticks?

Walkingsticks are some of the longest insects. They look like twigs!

Walkingsticks are also called stick insects. Their long, thin bodies are often green or brown.

ACTUAL SIZE:

northern walkingstick

Some walkingsticks have **spines** or bright wings. These scare away **predators**.

wing

Up in the Trees

Walkingsticks live in woods and **rain forests**. They climb trees and bushes.

Many stick insects are active at night. They look for tasty leaves.

FAVORITE FOOD:

leaves

13

During the day, walkingsticks are hidden in trees. They wave in the wind like twigs.

Growing Up

Female walkingsticks drop their eggs on the ground. The eggs look like seeds.

egg →

Nymphs climb trees after they **hatch**. They look for food.

hatching

WALKINGSTICK
LIFE SPAN:
up to 3 years

Nymphs **molt**
as they grow.
Soon the trees
are filled with
hidden insects!

molting

Glossary

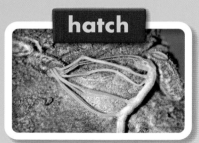

hatch

to break out of an egg

predators

animals that hunt other animals for food

molt

to shed skin for growth

rain forests

warm, wet forests that get a lot of rain

nymphs

young insects; nymphs look like small adults without full wings.

spines

sharp body parts that scare away predators

To Learn More

AT THE LIBRARY

Bestor, Sheri Mabry. *Good Trick, Walking Stick!*. Ann Arbor, Mich.: Sleeping Bear Press, 2016.

Bodden, Valerie. *Stick Insects*. Mankato, Minn.: Creative Education, 2014.

Carr, Aaron. *Stick Insects*. New York, N.Y.: AV2 by Weigl, 2015.

ON THE WEB

Learning more about walkingsticks is as easy as 1, 2, 3.

1. Go to www.factsurfer.com.

2. Enter "walkingsticks" into the search box.

3. Click the "Surf" button and you will see a list of related web sites.

With factsurfer.com, finding more information is just a click away.

Index

The images in this book are reproduced through the courtesy of: Thomas Marentant/ Pantheon/ SuperStock, front cover; IrinaK, pp. 4-5; Stephane Bidouze, pp. 6-7; Luc Viatour/ Wikipedia, pp. 8-9; Leonardo Mercon, pp. 10-11; Wildlife GmbH/ Alamy, pp. 12-13; alias612, p. 13; NNehring, pp. 14-15; mtcurado, pp. 16-17; Christian Hütter/ ImageBROKER/ SuperStock, pp. 18-19, 22 (hatch); Paul Starosta/ Getty Images, pp. 20-21 (walkingstick), 22 (molt); BlackOnyx7, pp. 20-21 (background); kurt_G, p. 22 (nymphs); Guillermo Guerao Serra, p. 22 (spines); Danita Delmont, p. 22 (predators); Fotos593, p. 22 (rain forests).

9